12/13

AMERICAN SPACE MISSIONS
ASTRONAUTS, EXPLORATION, AND DISCOVERY

Eye on the Universe
The Incredible Hubble Space Telescope

Michael D. Cole

Enslow Publishers, Inc.
40 Industrial Road
Box 398
Berkeley Heights, NJ 07922
USA

http://www.enslow.com

Original edition published as *Hubble Space Telescope: Exploring the Universe* in 1999.

Library of Congress Cataloging-in-Publication Data
Cole, Michael D.
  Eye on the universe : the incredible hubble space telescope / Michael D. Cole.
    p. cm. — (American space missions—Astronauts, exploration, and discovery)
  Rev. ed. of: Hubble space telescope / Michael D. Cole. 1999.
  Includes bibliographical references and index.
  ISBN 978-0-7660-4077-9
  1. Hubble Space Telescope (Spacecraft)—Juvenile literature. 2. Astronomy—Research—Juvenile literature. 3.
Astronautics in astronomy—Juvenile literature. I. Cole, Michael D. Hubble space telescope. II. Title.
  QB500.268.C65 2013
  522'.2919—dc23
                          2011047074
Future editions:
Paperback ISBN 978-1-4644-0074-2
ePUB ISBN 978-1-4645-0981-0
PDF ISBN 978-1-4646-0981-7

Printed in the United States of America

032012 Lake Book Manufacturing, Inc., Melrose Park, IL

10 9 8 7 6 5 4 3 2 1

To Our Readers: We have done our best to make sure all Internet addresses in this book were active and appropriate when we went to press. However, the author and the publisher have no control over and assume no liability for the material available on those Internet sites or on other Web sites they may link to. Any comments or suggestions can be sent by e-mail to comments@enslow.com or to the address on the back cover.

♻ Enslow Publishers, Inc., is committed to printing our books on recycled paper. The paper in every book contains 10% to 30% post-consumer waste (PCW). The cover board on the outside of each book contains 100% PCW. Our goal is to do our part to help young people and the environment too!

Illustration Credits: AP Images / NASA, pp. 11, 38, 41; NASA Goddard Space Flight Center, p. 32; NASA Goddard Space Flight Center / Space Telescope Science Institute, p. 40; NASA Johnson Space Center, pp. 1, 4, 16, 24; NASA Kennedy Space Center, p. 7; NASA Marshall Space Flight Center, pp. 9, 21, 22; STScI / NASA, pp. 13, 14, 19, 27, 34, 36, 42; Time & Life Pictures / Getty Images, p. 29.

Cover Illustration: NASA Johnson Space Center (Astronauts on spacewalk during the first repair mission for the Hubble Space Telescope in 1993).

Contents

Two astronauts repair the Hubble Space Telescope while it is docked with the space shuttle *Endeavour*.

CHAPTER 1

A Telescope Bound for Space

The Hubble Space Telescope was carefully loaded into the payload bay of the space shuttle *Discovery*. Astronomers, engineers, and other scientists had spent fifteen years designing and building the mighty telescope. At long last, it was ready for its journey into space. In the middle of April 1990, *Discovery* and its long-awaited cargo rolled slowly to the launchpad at Cape Canaveral, Florida.

The giant telescope had cost more than $1.6 billion! Scientists had faced many problems in constructing the telescope. Most of them believed their years of difficult effort were worth it. If the telescope worked, it would be the most powerful telescope ever built.

Finally, the day for which these scientists had long been waiting had arrived. *Discovery* sat on the launchpad with the Hubble Space Telescope inside, ready for its historic ride into space.

As the countdown continued, those who had worked on the telescope watched and listened. If all went well, *Discovery*'s crew of astronauts would release the telescope into orbit the following day. Strapped to their seats, the astronauts listened to the countdown on their helmet headsets.

T minus one minute and counting . . .

Like the thousands of people who had worked on the telescope, the astronauts braced themselves for the approaching moment of liftoff.

The final seconds ticked down.

Five . . . four . . . three . . . two . . . one . . .

Orange fire and huge clouds of smoke gushed outward from *Discovery*'s engines. The tremendous thrust lifted the space shuttle off the launchpad.

" . . . And liftoff of the space shuttle *Discovery*," the NASA announcer said, "with the Hubble Space Telescope—our window on the universe."[1]

Discovery roared through the sky toward space. As it climbed higher and higher, the solid rocket boosters and the external fuel tank separated from the shuttle. Minutes later, the shuttle was in orbit.

The next day, *Discovery*'s crew opened the payload bay doors. The Hubble Space Telescope, named after American astronomer Edwin Hubble, was then released into orbit around Earth.

It was more than three weeks before the telescope's instruments were ready to look at their first object in space. After all the waiting, astronomers had high hopes for this amazing machine.

Astronomers had long wanted a telescope in space. The biggest reason for such a telescope was simple: All light from space that reaches a telescope on the ground is blurred by Earth's atmosphere. A telescope in space, above Earth's atmosphere, would be able to see objects in space much more clearly. Without the blurring effect of Earth's atmosphere, it would also be able to see much farther out into space.

The most important part of the Hubble Space Telescope was an eight-foot-wide mirror. This primary mirror was designed to focus on distant objects in the universe like never before. Light from a distant star or galaxy would reflect off this large mirror and onto a series of smaller mirrors, bouncing the light into what was called the Wide Field Planetary Camera, or WF/PC. Because of this abbreviation, everyone called the camera the "wiff pic."[2]

Discovery lifts off from the launchpad at Cape Canaveral, Florida, on April 24, 1990, carrying the Hubble Space Telescope in its payload bay.

The WF/PC records the object's image and stores it in a computer. The computer then relays the image to the Space Telescope Science Institute in Baltimore, Maryland, where a team of astronomers studies it.

Many highly complex scientific instruments for measuring the mirror's reflected light were placed aboard the Hubble Space Telescope. The Faint-Object Camera was designed to take pictures of dim objects in space that can barely be seen from Earth. The Faint-Object Spectrograph would examine the different colors of light coming from these objects. By this method, scientists could learn the object's temperature, as well as its chemical and gas makeup.[3] The Goddard High-Resolution Spectrograph would look at objects in space, focusing on a special kind of radiation called ultraviolet light. Ultraviolet light is invisible to human eyes. The Hubble Space Telescope would give scientists a great new opportunity to observe this type of light from space.[4] The brightness of light coming from a star or galaxy would be measured by the High-Speed Photometer. This measurement would help astronomers learn about the size of the object in space, as well as its distance from Earth.

While the Hubble Space Telescope is a telescope, it is also a spacecraft. It is powered by a set of solar arrays attached to either side of the telescope. Its guidance system is used to point the telescope in the direction of the object scientists wish to view. This system is very important. The many powerful instruments aboard the Hubble would be useless if scientists were unable to aim and focus the telescope effectively.

HUBBLE SPACE TELESCOPE

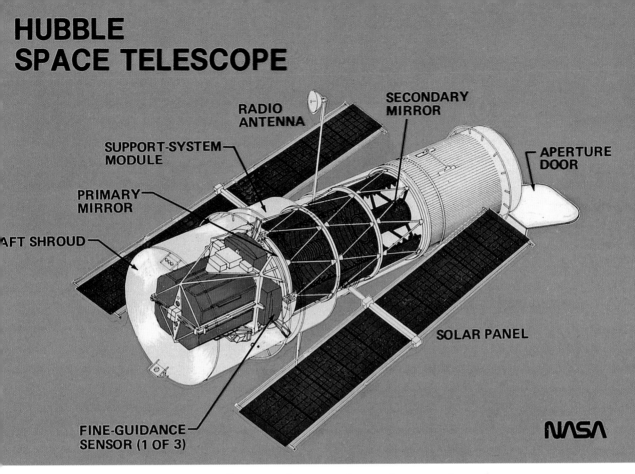

RADIO ANTENNA

SECONDARY MIRROR

SUPPORT-SYSTEM MODULE

APERTURE DOOR

PRIMARY MIRROR

AFT SHROUD

SOLAR PANEL

FINE-GUIDANCE SENSOR (1 OF 3)

NASA

Hubble, shown in this diagram, is not only a telescope, but also a spacecraft. Its guidance system allows scientists to point the telescope at objects they wish to view.

By May 20, 1990, the Hubble Space Telescope was ready to be aimed at its first target in space. The engineers, astronomers, and other scientists involved with the project believed the telescope's systems were ready for operation. Hundreds of these scientists gathered in control rooms at the Goddard Space Flight Center in Greenbelt, Maryland; the Marshall Space Flight Center in Huntsville, Alabama; and the Space Telescope Science Institute.

Reporters from newspapers and radio and television stations were there with the scientists to watch the first images from the new telescope. The press had carried many stories about the telescope during all the years it was being built. The public's expectations for the telescope were high.[5]

Controllers at the Goddard Space Flight Center sent a set of commands to the telescope. Orbiting 375 miles above Earth, the telescope responded, turning slowly to catch the light from a star cluster 1,300 light-years away. It was the star cluster NGC 3532.

The light from the distant star cluster hit the primary mirror, bounced up to the smaller secondary mirror, and traveled back through the central opening in the primary mirror. The twice-reflected light then bounced off another mirror and into the WF/PC, which recorded the image. All was going according to plan.

The scientists who had gathered at the three centers knew the telescope had received its aiming commands. For several minutes, all of them waited anxiously for the image to appear on their computer screens.[6]

The orbiting telescope then came into the range of a data relay satellite. The telescope sent its data to the satellite, and the satellite relayed them down to Earth. Computers at the Goddard Space Flight Center received the data and transformed them into a picture, which was seen by scientists, reporters, and engineers at the Space Telescope Science Institute as well.

In this photo, a robotic arm from *Discovery* holds the Hubble Space Telescope while it is being examined during its inaugural space flight. On May 20, 1990, Hubble was ready to take its first photograph.

A fuzzy group of stars appeared on the screen. People in the rooms grew excited as the camera team processed the image through a set of computer programs that slightly sharpened the picture.

"Look at that!" some of them shouted.

"It works! Hubble works!" said others.[7]

The press reported this first image from the Hubble Space Telescope as a great success. Astronomers and NASA officials told the reporters that they did not expect a sharp, clear picture from the telescope the first time it was used. NASA knew it would take days or even a few weeks to get all of the telescope's instruments adjusted properly.

However, as NASA adjusted the telescope, those days went by with no improvement in the images. No matter what they tried, the images remained blurry.

Weeks passed. The press wanted to know why the telescope was not yet producing amazing pictures of stars and galaxies. NASA scientists tried everything they knew to sharpen the images, but nothing worked.

When the telescope looked at a star, the image it produced had a bright point in the center surrounded by a strange blurry halo. NASA then put the telescope through a test that moved the primary mirror through its entire range of focus—very much like twisting the focus ring on a camera. As the primary mirror was moved from one end of its focus range to the other, it never produced a sharp picture.

This test led NASA scientists to a terrible conclusion: There was a flaw in the telescope's primary mirror.

The primary mirror had started out as a one-ton piece of optical-quality glass. Over a period of three years, two hundred pounds of the glass were carefully ground and polished away, until its shape was considered perfect to reflect the light from space. But something had gone wrong.

There was no way to ignore the evidence coming from Hubble. Scientists were stunned when they realized the problem was with the eight-foot primary mirror—the very heart of the telescope.

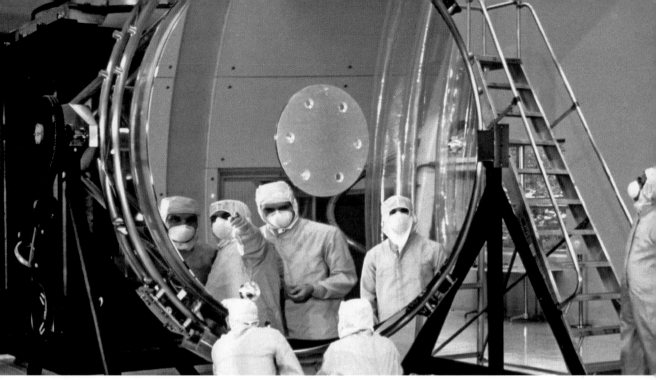

NASA scientists rejoiced when Hubble successfully transmitted its first image. However, weeks later, they still had been unable to focus the image. Soon, scientists discovered there was a flaw in the telescope's primary mirror. In this photo, workers study Hubble's eight-foot mirror prior to the launch in 1990.

The primary mirror had been ground and polished incorrectly. It suffered from what astronomers called a spherical aberration. One edge of the mirror was ten-thousandths of an inch too flat, a measurement one-fiftieth the width of a human hair. This measurement is invisible to the human eye.[8]

No matter how small the flaw, the result was that the telescope's mirror could not focus light into a sharp point.

The Hubble Space Telescope, the most powerful telescope ever built, could not be focused.

The high hopes for the Hubble Space Telescope had been shattered. The project quickly became a huge source of embarrassment to NASA.

A view of the Hubble Space Telescope prior to the launch in 1990. NASA spent $1.6 billion to build and launch Hubble, but the telescope still did not work properly. NASA needed to plan a daring repair mission in order to salvage the telescope.

The press harshly criticized them for the expensive failure. It was not long until the blurred space telescope became a source of jokes for comedians and cartoonists.

What could be done to fix a broken telescope that had already cost NASA $1.6 billion to build and launch into space? Scientists could not simply climb into it and fix it. It was in space, in orbit around Earth. The first scheduled mission to service the telescope was not for another four years!

The flaw in the primary mirror was not the telescope's only problem. As the telescope orbited from the light to the dark sides of Earth, the heating and cooling of the solar arrays caused the telescope to wobble. The guidance system was also having problems pointing the telescope at the correct objects in space.

NASA scientists began thinking of ideas that might solve the telescope's problems. Some at NASA wanted to capture the telescope with the shuttle and bring it back to Earth for repair. Others believed such a plan would not work. Once the telescope was back on the ground, they believed there would be no support from the public to repair it and get it back into space again.[9]

It was clear that a daring mission to repair the telescope in space would have to be planned.

NASA designed a complex repair mission and built special tools that scientists believed could be used to correct the focus of the primary mirror and fix the guidance system.

Only a repair in space could save the Hubble Space Telescope.

NASA's ambitious mission to repair the Hubble Space Telescope required a team of astronauts to fly into space and make the repairs manually. A space shuttle carrying the astronauts would have to dock with the telescope as it orbited the Earth.

CHAPTER 2

Hubble Trouble

As NASA discovered each new problem with the telescope, scientists worked hard at finding ways to solve it. If a problem could not be corrected from the ground, it became part of the planning for the repair mission. The solution to some of these problems involved designing and building new instruments that could be installed aboard the telescope. Installing these new instruments would be the work of a team of astronauts on NASA's first repair mission in space.

Detailed plans for the mission to repair the Hubble Space Telescope began in the summer of 1990. The long list of repairs took shape through 1991 and most of 1992. Because of the huge cost of these repairs, the stakes for the repair mission were high. NASA's reputation, and possibly its future, was on the line. Much would be gained by the mission's success, and much would be lost if it failed.

For the all-important mission, NASA selected one of the most experienced crews of astronauts it had ever assembled. Their training began more than a year before the mission, which was scheduled to launch in December 1993.

"I'm not overconfident," said astronaut Story Musgrave. "I'm running scared." Musgrave was the mission's payload commander, and he was responsible for coordinating the spacewalks that would repair the telescope. He knew how difficult a job the mission was going to be for him and the crew. "This thing is frightening to me. I'm looking for every kind of thing that might get out and bite us."[1]

Musgrave had been a surgeon before he came to NASA. When asked why he gave up surgery to become an astronaut, he quickly answered, "Why, so I could operate on the Hubble, of course."[2]

Dick Covey was the mission commander, in charge of the overall success and safety of the mission. Kenneth Bowersox, whom everyone called Sox, would back up Covey as shuttle pilot.

Mission specialist Claude Nicollier would operate the shuttle's robotic arm, or Remote Manipulator System (RMS). He would use the arm to grab and release the telescope. During the repairs, a fellow astronaut would be attached to the end of the arm. Nicollier would move the astronaut around the shuttle's payload bay in the same way a firefighter is moved when in the bucket of a cherry picker.

Two teams of spacewalkers would make the repairs to the telescope. Musgrave's spacewalking partner would be mission specialist Jeffrey Hoffman. The other spacewalking team would be mission specialists Thomas Akers and Kathryn "K.T." Thornton. All four had conducted spacewalks on previous missions.

The team of astronauts chosen for the daring repair mission had to undergo extensive training. In this photo, astronauts Steven Smith and John Grunsfeld train in the Goddard Space Flight Center, working on a backup of an electrical section of Hubble for a servicing mission in 1999. The astronauts are wearing special suits to protect the sensitive equipment from particles that could interfere with its performance.

After months of exhaustive training, the team of astronauts was ready for the mission. In the darkness at 1:00 A.M. on December 2, 1993, the crew rode to the launchpad at the Kennedy Space Center in Florida and climbed aboard the space shuttle *Endeavour*. Strapped into their seats, they waited through the countdown as the launch drew nearer. Once again, everyone involved with the Hubble Space Telescope was watching closely.

Endeavour sat on the launchpad, lit up with spotlights. Only seconds to go before liftoff.

"Ten . . . nine . . . eight . . . seven . . . and GO for main engine start," said the public-address announcer. "Five . . . four . . . three . . . two . . . one." At 4:27 A.M., the shuttle's engines ignited, lighting up the night as it thundered off the pad into the early morning sky. "And we have liftoff . . . liftoff of the space shuttle *Endeavour* and an ambitious mission to service the Hubble Space Telescope."[3]

In a matter of minutes, *Endeavour* and its crew were in orbit around Earth. They were now chasing the telescope. Over the next two days, *Endeavour* would gradually close the distance between them. The astronauts spent this period checking all the shuttle's systems and getting used to the sensation of weightlessness.

Early on the third day, *Endeavour*'s crew caught its first sight of Hubble. Commander Dick Covey and pilot Ken Bowersox guided the shuttle closer to the telescope.

"Now it's all eyeballs and hands," Bowersox said.[4] He knew the control thrusters of the shuttle had only enough fuel for one try at getting close enough to the telescope. They had to get it right.

Claude Nicollier took his place at the controls of the robotic arm. *Endeavour* drew closer and closer to the telescope. Nicollier reached out with the arm, and its claw gently grasped the Hubble Space Telescope.

Commander Covey said to Mission Control: "*Endeavour* has a firm handshake with Mr. Hubble's telescope."[5] Covey's announcement caused a sigh of relief in the Mission Control room. The telescope was

Astronauts Story Musgrave and Jeffrey Hoffman were tasked with the mission's first spacewalk to repair the telescope's faulty gyroscopes. This photo taken from *Endeavour* on December 2, 1993, shows Musgrave during his spacewalk.

Astronauts Story Musgrave and Jeffrey Hoffman, perched atop foot restraints attached to *Endeavour*'s robotic arm, repair Hubble during a spacewalk. The two astronauts had no trouble replacing the gyroscopes, but struggled to get the panel doors closed at the bottom of the telescope.

in place in the shuttle's payload bay. The long and challenging task of repairing the telescope could now begin.

The following day, Story Musgrave and Jeffrey Hoffman helped each other slide into their cumbersome space suits for the repair mission's first spacewalk. Their task was to replace the telescope's faulty gyroscopes. Gyroscopes are instruments that are used to keep vehicles such as boats, airplanes, and spacecraft steady. The telescope needed the gyroscopes to keep it steady when scientists pointed it in the direction where they wanted to look. Three of the telescope's six gyroscopes had failed and needed to be replaced.

Musgrave and Hoffman entered the air lock and closed the hatch behind them. The air lock is a room in which air pressure is slowly reduced to what the astronauts experience outside the protection of the shuttle. This had to occur before they opened the other hatch and floated out into space. The astronauts kept themselves attached to the payload bay by metal cables. Musgrave slowly made his way toward the telescope, which stood upright at the rear of the payload bay. Hoffman attached his feet to the end of the robotic arm. Nicollier then moved Hoffman and the arm toward the telescope.

Musgrave and Hoffman opened the panel doors near the bottom of the telescope. The two astronauts worked well together and had no problem replacing the gyroscope mechanisms. But when they were finished, Musgrave discovered he could not get the panel doors shut again. One of the doors was sagging.

In this photo, astronaut Kathryn Thornton releases the old solar array into space during the Hubble repair mission. After discarding the broken instrument, Thornton and Thomas Akers installed the new solar arrays to the telescope.

They tried different tools to force the doors shut but none of them worked. Musgrave suggested using something called a come-along. This tool had a crank that would pull the doors together and hold them. With the come-along holding the doors together, Musgrave used his hands to push them shut.[6]

The incident with the doors showed the astronauts that not everything would go perfectly. They would have to be clever and resourceful to overcome some of the mission's unexpected problems.

Musgrave and Hoffman's next task was to prepare the equipment for the removal of the solar arrays on either side of the telescope. The arrays were designed to roll up like window blinds. The first array rolled up perfectly. The other array had been warped. It would not roll up. The safest thing to do with the broken array was to throw it out into space, away from the shuttle. That job would be done the following day by Tom Akers and Kathy Thornton.

Akers and Thornton pulled on their space suits and went to work on the mission's second spacewalk. Thornton was at the end of the robotic arm. She steadied the solar array while Akers disconnected it. He had to be very careful not to bend the pins that held the electrical connectors. If they were bent, they could not be used to attach the new solar arrays. Without the solar arrays, the telescope would have no power.

Akers slowly and carefully disconnected each bolt and pin as the shuttle orbited into Earth's night side. Finally, the solar array was free. Thornton alone held the solar array. She had to hold it perfectly still. If it began to move around, it could hit the telescope and damage it. While Thornton held the array, Nicollier used the robotic arm to move her and the array slowly away from the telescope.

"OK, Claude, real easy," she said.[7]

At that moment, they were still on the night side of Earth. They needed to wait until daylight when the entire crew could see clearly, in case the solar array threatened to float back against the telescope when it was released. Thornton had to hold the solar array at the end of the robotic arm for several minutes, waiting for daylight. As *Endeavour* orbited onward, Thornton's partner finally saw light appear on Earth's horizon.

"I think I see sunrise coming, K.T.," Akers said.[8]

Endeavour and its spacewalkers orbited into daylight.

"OK, Tom," Musgrave said from inside the shuttle. "Tell K.T. to go for release."

"OK, K.T. You ready?" Akers asked.

"Ready," Thornton said.

"Got a go for release," Akers said.[9]

At that moment, Thornton released both of her hands from the array. "OK. No hands," Thornton said. Bowersox immediately used *Endeavour*'s control thrusters to steer the shuttle away from the floating solar array. The crew watched as the solar array floated safely away from the shuttle.[10] The solar array would stay in orbit for some time before eventually burning up in Earth's atmosphere.

Thornton and Akers successfully attached the new solar arrays. They crawled back inside the shuttle for a well-deserved rest.

The third spacewalk was an important one. The task for Musgrave and Hoffman this time was to replace the Wide Field Planetary Camera, or WF/PC, with an improved version called WF/PC 2. This was probably the most delicate operation of the mission.

Hoffman held the large camera in his hands as he stood at the end of the robotic arm. He had to hold the camera very steady while Musgrave carefully removed the protective cover from the mirror. The mirror of the new camera was just several inches from the faceplate of Musgrave's helmet. If he touched or bumped the exposed mirror even slightly, the mirror would be knocked out of alignment—a disaster that would ruin the camera before it ever took its first picture.

Astronauts Story Musgrave and Jeffrey Hoffman were charged with the most intricate operation of the mission: replacing the Wide Field Planetary Camera with an improved version, WF/PC 2. This photo shows one of the astronauts removing the old camera during the repair mission.

Musgrave moved out of the way slowly and precisely. He then helped Hoffman guide WF/PC 2 snugly into its slot in the telescope. The camera was in place, and the third spacewalk was another success.

It was Akers and Thornton's turn again. Their task for the fourth spacewalk was to install a device that was of central importance to the telescope. It was called COSTAR, which stood for Corrective Optics Space Telescope Axial Replacement. This was the device that scientists had designed to correct the flaw in the telescope's primary mirror.

COSTAR was a metal box the size of a refrigerator. It contained a set of ten movable mirrors, each of which was no larger than a thumbnail.[11] Once COSTAR was installed in the telescope, it would deploy these mirrors. The mirrors would reflect the primary mirror's light in a way that would correct its flaw. In other words, although they could not correct the primary mirror itself, they could correct the path of light reflected from it.

Nicollier guided Thornton forward at the end of the robotic arm, where she held COSTAR in her hands. However, it was so big that she could not see where she was going. Akers served as her eyes. He hummed as he helped Thornton guide the mechanism into place. Nicollier was listening at the controls of the robotic arm.

"It was good to hear Tom humming," Nicollier said later, "because we knew when Tom was humming things were going well. And Tom was humming most of the time!"[12]

Akers and Thornton slid COSTAR into its tight fit inside the telescope. The major repairs of the mission were completed. They were almost home free.

On the fifth and final spacewalk, there was a bit of drama. Musgrave and Hoffman were wrapping up the repairs when a small screw escaped from Musgrave's tool bag. If it was lost, there could be trouble. The space shuttle is a complex machine. Even something as small as a loose screw floating inside the shuttle's payload bay during reentry could spell serious disaster.

They had to catch the screw. Musgrave was attached to the end of the robotic arm, and Hoffman was tethered to it. But the screw was floating down and away from them into the payload bay, where it would become impossible to find. Nicollier saw the screw's glinting light from his place at the robotic arm's controls. He quickly began to guide

Astronaut Kathy Thornton services equipment on the Hubble Space Telescope during the fourth spacewalk of the repair mission. Her task during this operation, along with **Tom Akers**, was to install **COSTAR**, the device that would correct the flaw in the telescope's primary mirror.

Hoffman and Musgrave down in its direction. Nicollier was moving the arm much faster than usual, because he knew it was important to capture the tumbling screw.

Hoffman reached out his hand as they chased it. Down and down toward the payload bay they went.

Just as Hoffman's feet were about to bump into the side of the payload bay, he caught it. "I have it," he said.

"Okay, arm stop," Musgrave said quickly.[13]

The screw was returned to the bag. With a sigh of relief, Musgrave and Hoffman went about their work and completed the repairs.

On the following day, the newly repaired Hubble Space Telescope was released back into orbit. The crew of *Endeavour* had done their best on the telescope. They had conducted five spacewalks—more spacewalks than any other American astronauts or Russian cosmonauts had ever conducted on any single mission. It was an impressive record. After eleven successful days in space, they were ready to come home.

Endeavour made a night landing at the Kennedy Space Center in Florida. As far as the astronauts knew, nothing had gone wrong on their mission. But they did not yet know if their mission had been a success.

NASA scientists and astronomers around the world once again focused their attention on the Hubble Space Telescope. All waited to see if the repairs had worked.

CHAPTER 3

Hubble's Second Chance

A few days after *Endeavour*'s astronauts had returned to Earth, a group of scientists and astronomers gathered at the Space Telescope Science Institute. Although the *Endeavour* mission had appeared to be flawless, no one would know for sure if the repairs were successful until the telescope was fully tested. It was the first day of those important tests, the day the telescope would produce its first images from the new WF/PC 2.

The new corrective optics were delicately deployed inside the telescope. Scientists at the institute waited anxiously as power was fed to the telescope's other controls and instruments.[1] Everything looked good as it moved through a series of checkout commands. The new gyroscopes reacted as the telescope was pointed at a distant star called AGK +81 D226.[2]

Again the telescope recorded the image in its computers. Minutes passed as the telescope's orbit carried it around Earth and into the range of the relay satellite.

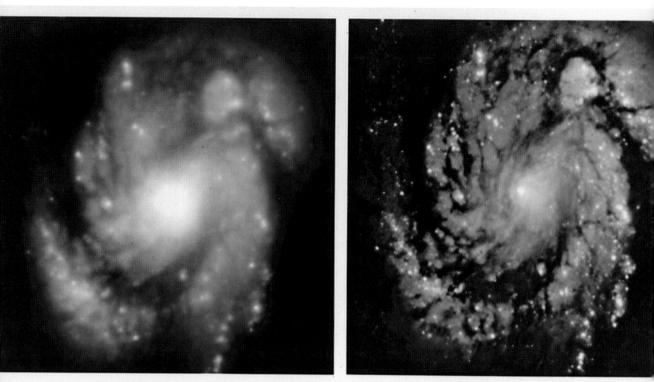

Wide Field Planetary Camera 1

Wide Field Planetary Camera 2

This comparison image of the core of galaxy M100 shows the amazing improvement in Hubble Space Telescope's view of the universe after the first repair mission in 1993.

Scientists in the control room watched their monitor. Light surged through the screen. There was a momentary flicker before the image steadied.

A silence fell over the room as the image from space appeared. There on the screen was the clear, sharp picture of their targeted star!

Cheers and applause erupted throughout the room. Scientists shook hands and slapped each other's backs. The new picture was fantastic. The repaired telescope was working beyond their wildest expectations. It was a joyous moment for them all.[3]

The new instruments skillfully installed during the daring repair mission were tremendously successful. The Hubble Space Telescope was finally able to photograph distant objects in space with a clarity ten times greater than the most powerful telescopes on Earth.

Work with the Hubble Space Telescope was only beginning.

In February 1997, another team of astronauts was sent into space to make further improvements to the telescope. Ken Bowersox, who had been the shuttle pilot on the repair mission in 1993, was the commander on this mission aboard the space shuttle *Discovery*. Bowersox and his crew removed the Faint-Object Spectrograph and installed the Near-Infrared Camera and Multi-Object Spectrometer, or NICMOS. NICMOS photographs and measures the infrared wavelengths of light from objects in the universe. Infrared wavelengths cannot be detected by the human eye.

The 1997 *Discovery* mission also installed the Space Telescope Imaging Spectrograph to make more sensitive studies of ultraviolet light from objects in space. The astronauts also replaced one of the three guidance sensors and a number of other components aboard the telescope.

The 1993 repair mission and the 1997 servicing mission have put the Hubble Space Telescope in excellent working condition. With the telescope's continuing use by astronomers—and more improvements planned for the future—it may help us answer some of our most important questions about the universe.

An astronaut removes the Faint-Object Spectrograph before installing the Near-Infrared Camera and Multi-Object Spectrometer during the servicing mission in 1997.

The Hubble Space Telescope is sometimes described as both a telescope and a time machine. This is because the telescope may be able to tell us how old the universe is.

How?

Astronomers measure the vast distances in our universe by light-years. A light-year is the distance that light will travel through space in one year. Light travels at the incredible speed of 186,000 miles per second. Light, moving at that speed, will travel 5.9 trillion miles in a single year. One light-year, then, equals 5.9 trillion miles.

Our own solar system lies 25,000 light-years from the center of our Milky Way galaxy. That seems like a great distance in space. However, the Hubble Space Telescope, after its repairs in 1993, is able to see 13 billion light-years away!

The important thing to remember is this: The light reaching us from that distance has been traveling 13 billion years. The telescope's picture of a galaxy 13 billion light-years away is not a picture of how that galaxy appears now. It is a picture of how that galaxy appeared 13 billion years ago, when those light rays began their journey to us.

In this way, the Hubble Space Telescope serves as a time machine. The greater the distance the telescope sees into space, the farther it sees into the past.

It may one day be able to see almost to the beginning of the universe. Such discoveries may help astronomers learn how the universe was formed.

The large Whirlpool Galaxy (left) is known for its sharply defined spiral arms that could be the result of its gravitational tug-of-war with its smaller companion galaxy (right). The Hubble Space Telescope can capture images of stars and galaxies that are billions of light years away from Earth.

The Hubble Space Telescope is an amazing tool for astronomers. Astronaut Story Musgrave, who risked his life in the spacewalks to repair the Hubble, understood that the telescope may answer questions about the universe that are important to us all.

"It is a reach out there for the heavens," he said, "to find out what this universe is all about."[4]

CHAPTER 4

The Tip of the Iceberg

On February 1, 2003, tragedy occurred when the space shuttle *Columbia* exploded after reentering Earth's atmosphere. All seven astronauts on board were killed. As a result, NASA grounded its shuttle fleet. This meant the Hubble could not be serviced. It would be almost three years before NASA announced a new service mission for the Hubble telescope.

In all, three more servicing missions took place on the Hubble between 1999 and 2009. Service included replacing gyroscopes, adding new solar arrays, and computer updates. The 2009 mission also added two new instruments: the Wide Field Camera 3 and the Cosmic Origins Spectrograph. This last mission was expected to keep the Hubble functioning through at least 2014.[1]

The most recent improvements on the Hubble made it more powerful than ever. Research and discoveries related to the telescope's observations continued at an incredible pace. Through August 2011,

Astronauts work on the Hubble
Space Telescope during the
servicing mission on May 14, 2009.
This mission was expected to keep
Hubble functioning until 2014.

more than nine thousand papers based on Hubble data had been published.[2] This is a greater output of work than any other modern scientific instrument has prompted.[3]

The Hubble helped solve many mysteries of the universe, as well as confirm other theories long held by scientists. For example, it was widely accepted that any large galaxy would have a black hole at its center. However, the centers of most galaxies are packed so tight with stars that we cannot see them clearly with an Earth telescope. But the Hubble can see and track these individual stars. The velocity of these stars makes it clear that a black hole is attracting them.[4]

One of the great mysteries that had puzzled scientists throughout the ages is this: How old is the universe? The answer to this question has been largely answered, thanks to both the Hubble telescope and the scientist for whom the telescope was named.

In 1929, Edwin Hubble came up with the formula for what we now call Hubble's law. This law says (basically) that the velocity of objects moving in space and their distance from other objects is proportional. In theory, Hubble's law should have allowed scientists to determine the age of the universe. But for many years, we lacked accurate data. Some scientists thought the universe was about 10 billion years old, while others contended that it was 20 billion years old.[5] Thanks to the Hubble telescope, we finally have data accurate enough to tell the age of the universe. We can now say (with a margin for error of about 1 percent) that the universe was born 13.7 billion years ago.[6]

The magnificent images that Hubble captures and the unique data it provides have helped solve many mysteries of the universe. This image created from three separate photos taken by Hubble shows a column of molecular hydrogen gas and dust that is an incubator for new stars. The stars are embedded inside the finger-like bulges at the top of the column.

The Hubble has also helped us learn more about our own galaxy. It brought us our first clear images of Pluto and detected a thin atmosphere of oxygen around Europa, one of Jupiter's moons. It also recorded a huge storm on the planet Saturn that was so big it was larger than our planet Earth! The Hubble even helped us to predict the weather on Mars when the NASA mission of *Pathfinder* was sent there in 1997.

It was also in July 1997 that the Hubble discovered a young galaxy 13 billion light-years away. The following month, the telescope recorded what may be the first image of a planet there. This would be the first planet discovered outside of our solar system.[7]

The Hubble Space Telescope celebrated its twentieth birthday on April 22, 2010. To commemorate the occasion, NASA, the European

This photo shows the giant planet Jupiter with one of its moons, Ganymede (right). The Hubble Space Telescope has given scientists clear images and important data about planets in our galaxy.

Space Agency (ESA), and the Space Telescope Institute (STScI) released an image from the Carina Nebula.[8] The following year, the telescope made its one millionth observation.[9]

It was also early in 2011 that it was reported the telescope had observed what is likely the farthest galaxy yet discovered. This tiny

A view of Messier 81, a spiral galaxy similar to the Milky Way, from the Hubble Space Telescope. This is one of the brightest galaxies seen from Earth. Hubble has also allowed scientists to study galaxies far from our planet. In 2011, Hubble observed the farthest-known galaxy, a tiny speck of light that has been traveling toward Earth for 13.2 billion years.

speck of light has been traveling to us for about 13.2 billion years—which means it began when the universe was less than a half-billion years old. This is about 4 percent of the universe's current age.[10]

"In essence, the most important aspect of this is, it provides us with some sense of how fast galaxies are building up," said Dr. Rychard J. Bouwens of the University of California, Santa Cruz. "It provides a sort of measuring stick."[11]

Based on this latest discovery, Bouwens and his team concluded that the birthrate of stars increased tenfold between the time of this galaxy and that of the next, earliest-known galaxy (about 150 million years later). This is faster than most astronomers had previously believed.[12]

The next and final mission for the Hubble will be to deorbit the telescope, as it will have reached the end of its service life. Its scientific successor, the James Webb Space Telescope (JWST), is currently due to be launched by 2018. The JWST is poised to take us even farther than the Hubble has. It has been specially designed to reach these deep galaxies that the Hubble can only offer the tiniest glimpse.

"We really are not probing faint enough with the current Hubble observations to see beyond the tip of the iceberg," said Dr. Bouwens.[13]

It is amazing to consider that as much as we have learned from the Hubble and as far as it has taken science, there is still so much further to go. The wonders and mysteries of the universe seem truly endless.

Chapter Notes

Chapter 1. A Telescope Bound for Space

1. Carolyn Collins Petersen and John C. Brandt, *Hubble Vision: Astronomy With the Hubble Space Telescope* (New York: Cambridge University Press, 1995), p. 33.
2. Elaine Scott and Margaret Miller, *Adventure in Space: The Flight to Fix the Hubble* (New York: Hyperion Books for Children, 1995), p. 10.
3. Robert W. Smith, *The Space Telescope: A Study of NASA, Science, Technology, and Politics* (New York: Cambridge University Press, 1989), pp. 245–246, 253–256.
4. Petersen and Brandt, p. 68.
5. Ibid., p. 3.
6. Ibid., pp. 2–3.
7. Ibid., pp. 3–5.
8. Jay Barbree and Martin Caidin, *A Journey Through Time: Exploring the Universe With the Hubble Space Telescope* (New York: Penguin Books, 1995), p. xii.
9. *Rescue Mission in Space: The Hubble Space Telescope*, NOVA Adventures in Science, 1994 (video).

Chapter 2. Hubble Trouble

1. Elaine Scott and Margaret Miller, *Adventure in Space: The Flight to Fix the Hubble* (New York: Hyperion Books for Children, 1995), p. 5.
2. Ibid., p. 13.
3. *Rescue Mission in Space: The Hubble Space Telescope*, NOVA Adventures in Science, 1994 (video).
4. Scott and Miller, p. 48.
5. NOVA video.
6. Scott and Miller, p. 51.
7. Ibid., pp. 52–53.
8. Ibid., p. 53.
9. Ibid.
10. NOVA video.
11. Jay Barbree and Martin Caidin, *A Journey Through Time: Exploring the Universe With the Hubble Space Telescope* (New York: Penguin Books, 1995), p. xiv.
12. Scott and Miller, p. 55.
13. NOVA video.

Chapter 3. Hubble's Second Chance

1. Carolyn Collins Petersen and John C. Brandt, *Hubble Vision: Astronomy With the Hubble Space Telescope* (New York: Cambridge University Press, 1995), pp. 43–44.
2. Jay Barbree and Martin Caidin, *A Journey Through Time: Exploring the Universe With the Hubble Space Telescope* (New York: Penguin Books, 1995), p. xix.
3. Ibid.
4. *Rescue Mission in Space: The Hubble Space Telescope*, NOVA Adventures in Science, 1994 (video).

Chapter 4. The Tip of the Iceberg

1. "Space Topics: Hubble Space Telescope Historical Timeline," *The Planetary Society*, 2011, <http://www.planetary.org/explore/topics/hubble/history.html> (August 20, 2011).
2. "HST Publication Statistics," *The Multimission Archive at STScI*, April 14, 2011, <http://archive.stsci.edu/hst/bibliography/pubstat.html> (August 20, 2011).
3. Neil deGrasse Tyson, "For the Love of Hubble," *Parade*, June 22, 2008, <http://www.parade.com/articles/editions/2008/edition_06-22-2008/1New_View_of_Space> (August 20, 2011).
4. Ibid.
5. Ibid.
6. "How Old Is the Universe?" *WMAP Site*, July 19, 2010, <http://map.gsfc.nasa.gov/universe/uni_age.html> (August 20, 2011).
7. Malcolm W. Browne, "Image Is Believed to Be the First of a Planet Beyond Solar System," *The New York Times*, May 29, 1998, p. A1.
8. "Starry-Eyed Hubble Celebrates 20 Years of Awe and Discovery," *Hubblesite*, April 22, 2010, <http://hubblesite.org/newscenter/archive/releases/2010/13/> (August 17, 2011).
9. "Timeline," *The Hubble European Space Agency Information Centre*, 2011, <http://www.spacetelescope.org/about/history/timeline/> (August 21, 2011).
10. Mike Wall, "Oldest Galaxy: Hubble Telescope Detects Farthest, Oldest Galaxy Yet," *The Christian Science Monitor*, January 26, 2011, <http://www.csmonitor.com/Science/2011/0126/Oldest-galaxy-Hubble-telescope-detects-farthest-oldest-galaxy-yet> (August 21, 2011).
11. Dennis Overbye, "In Hubble's Lens, Signs of a Galaxy Older and Farther Than Any Other," *The New York Times*, January 26, 2011, <http://www.nytimes.com/2011/01/27/science/space/27galaxy.html> (August 21, 2011).
12. Ibid.
13. Ibid.

Glossary

COSTAR—Corrective Optics Space Telescope Axial Replacement. The instrument placed inside the Hubble Space Telescope to correct the flaw in the telescope's primary mirror.

deploy—To move an object, such as a satellite, into position.

Faint-Object Camera—Unique camera aboard the Hubble Space Telescope that takes pictures of exceptionally faint objects too dim to be seen by telescopes on Earth. It was developed by the European Space Agency, an important contributor to the telescope project.

Goddard High-Resolution Spectrograph—Instrument aboard the Hubble Space Telescope that analyzes ultraviolet light from glowing objects in space.

guidance system—The system aboard the Hubble Space Telescope that points it in the direction scientists wish to view.

gyroscope—A spinning device used to stabilize vehicles such as boats, planes, or spacecraft. They are an important part of the Hubble Space Telescope's guidance system.

High-Speed Photometer—Instrument aboard the Hubble Space Telescope that can measure the size or magnitude of a star and its distance from Earth.

light-year—A measure of distance used by astronomers. Light travels at 186,000 miles per second, covering a distance of 5.9 trillion miles in one year. Therefore, 5.9 trillion miles equals one light-year.

optical telescope assembly—The central component of the Hubble Space Telescope, consisting of the primary and secondary mirror construction.

payload bay—The area of the space shuttle where cargo is stored.

Remote Manipulator System—The robotic arm in the payload bay of the space shuttle. It is controlled from the rear of the shuttle's flight deck and was a major tool in the repair of the Hubble Space Telescope.

solar array—Silicon panels that use light from the sun to generate electrical power. The Hubble Space Telescope is powered by two solar arrays.

spectrograph—An instrument that divides light rays or other forms of radiation into a spectrum and then records that spectrum.

spherical aberration—Defect in the curvature of an optical mirror, preventing light from being focused into a single point.

ultraviolet—A part of the light spectrum that is invisible to human eyes. Most ultraviolet light from space is absorbed by Earth's atmosphere.

Wide Field Planetary Camera—Camera aboard the Hubble Space Telescope that takes pictures of wider areas of the sky than the Faint-Object Camera. It can also narrow its field of vision to take detailed pictures of nearby objects such as planets, asteroids, and comets.

Further Reading

Books

Devorkin, David, and Robert W. Smith. *Hubble: Imaging Space and Time.* Washington, D.C.: Smithsonian National Air and Space Museum in association with National Geographic, 2008.

Jefferis, David. *Star Spotters: Telescopes and Observatories.* New York: Crabtree Publishing, 2009.

Kupperberg, Paul. *Hubble and the Big Bang.* New York: Rosen Publishing Group, 2005.

Scott, Elaine. *Space, Stars, and the Beginning of Time: What the Hubble Telescope Saw.* Boston: Clarion Books, 2011.

Internet Addresses

European Space Agency (ESA): Hubble
  <http://www.spacetelescope.org/>

HubbleSite
  <http://hubblesite.org/>

NASA: The Hubble Space Telescope
  <http://hubble.nasa.gov/>

Index